First Guide to Maps

Reading Maps

**Marta Segal Block and
Daniel R. Block**

Raintree

www.raintreepublishers.co.uk

Visit our website to find out more information about Raintree books.

To order:

☎ Phone 0845 6044371

🗐 Fax +44 (0) 1865 312263

🖳 Email myorders@capstonepub.co.uk

Customers from outside the UK please telephone +44 1865 312262

Raintree is an imprint of Capstone Global Library Limited, a company incorporated in England and Wales having its registered office at 7 Pilgrim Street, London, EC4V 6LB – Registered company number: 6695582

Raintree is a registered trademark of Pearson Education Limited, under licence to Capstone Global Library Limited

Editorial: Cassie Mayer and Sian Smith
Design: Jennifer Lacki, Kimberly R. Miracle, and Betsy Wernert
Production: Duncan Gilbert

Illustrated by Mapping specialists
Originated by Modern Age
Printed and bound in China by South China Printing Co. Ltd

ISBN: 978 0 431 12782 8
12 11 10
10 9 8 7 6 5 4 3 2

British Library Cataloguing in Publication Data

Block, Marta Segal

Reading maps. - (First guide to maps)

1. Map reading - Juvenile literature 2. Cartography - Juvenile literature 3. Maps - Juvenile literature

I. Title II. Block, Daniel, 1967-

912'.014

Acknowledgements

The author and publishers are grateful to the following for permission to reproduce copyright material: ©Corbis pp. **10** (zefa/ Jason Horowitz); **13b** (Royalty Free); ©drr. net/Stock Connection p. **9** (Mark & Audrey Gibson); ©Getty Images pp. **12a** (Royalty Free), **13a** (Royalty Free); ©istockphoto pp. **12b** (Björn Kindler), **27** (roberta casaliggi); ©Map Resources p. **4**; ©NASA p. **26**.

Cover design by Kimberly R. Miracle and Jennifer Lacki

Every effort has been made to contact copyright holders of any material reproduced in this book. Any omissions will be rectified in subsequent printings if notice is given to the publishers.

Disclaimer

All the Internet addresses (URLs) given in this book were valid at the time of going to press. However, due to the dynamic nature of the Internet, some addresses may have changed, or sites may have changed or ceased to exist since publication. While the author and publisher regret any inconvenience this may cause readers, no responsibility for any such changes can be accepted by either the author or the publisher.

Contents

Any words appearing in the text in bold, **like this**, are explained in the glossary.

What are maps?

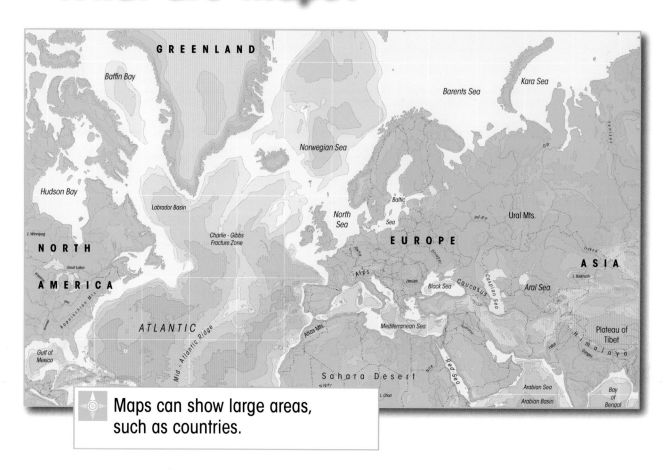

Maps can show large areas, such as countries.

A map is a flat drawing of a part of the world. People who make maps are called **cartographers**.

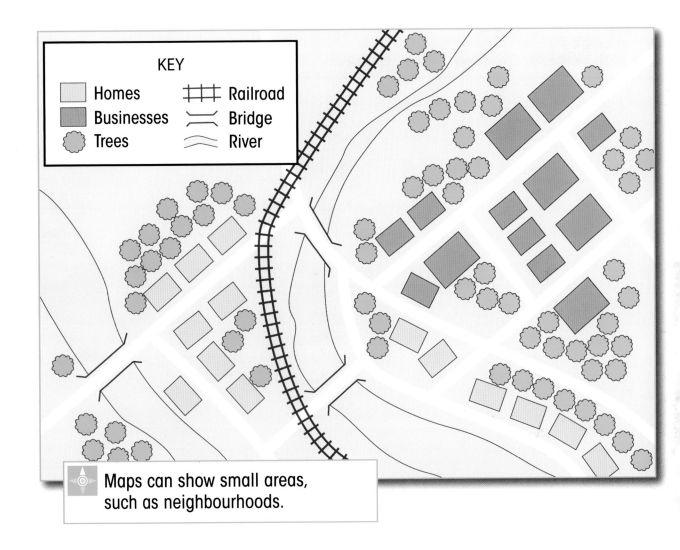

KEY

Homes		Railroad	
Businesses		Bridge	
Trees		River	

Maps can show small areas, such as neighbourhoods.

We use maps to find the location of places. We use them to study physical features such as mountains or lakes. We also use them to learn more about people.

Types of maps

Some maps show physical features of the land. They show the location of mountains, valleys, rivers, and lakes. These are called physical maps.

This is a map of the physical features of the world.

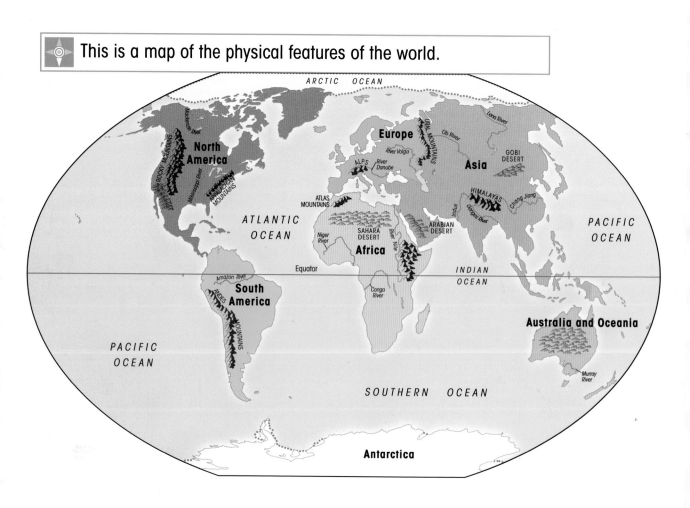

This map shows how many people live in South America.

Some maps show information about people and where they live. They show the location of cities, roads, and airports. They show the **borders** between countries. They can also show how many people live in an area.

Fitting the Earth onto a map

You may wonder how mapmakers fit the round Earth on a flat map. Try this activity: Use a pen to draw some lines and circles on the skin of an orange. Now peel the orange and try to make the skin of the orange lay flat. Notice how the size and shape of your drawings have changed. You have to push and pull the peel to flatten it.

To fit the Earth's features onto a map, **cartographers** "push" and "pull" in a similar way. They change the shape and size of things on the Earth. Then they can fit them onto a map.

Cartographers choose which features of the Earth they must change to fit them onto a map.

Reading maps

Maps have many features that help you to read them.

Map title

Most maps have a title. The title tells you what the map is about. The title could be the name of a location. It could also tell you about the type of information shown.

Compass rose

Many maps have a **compass rose**. This feature shows the **cardinal directions**. The cardinal directions are north, south, east, and west.

Milton town centre

Map symbols

Maps have many different **symbols**. Symbols are small pictures or shapes that represent things in real life. Dots and lines are common map symbols.

Dots often represent cities. Lines on a map may represent roads.

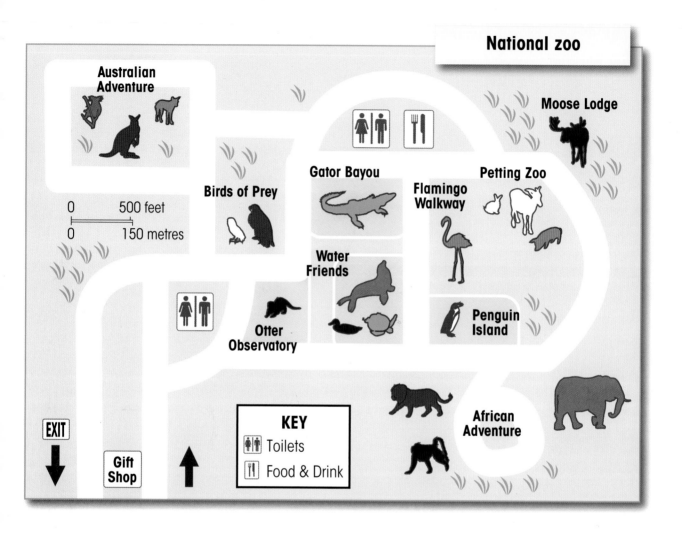

Some **symbols** on a map look like the things they represent. On the map above, pictures of animals show their location in a zoo.

Map key

Symbols can be different from map to map. That is why maps have a **key**. This feature tells you what the symbols on the map mean.

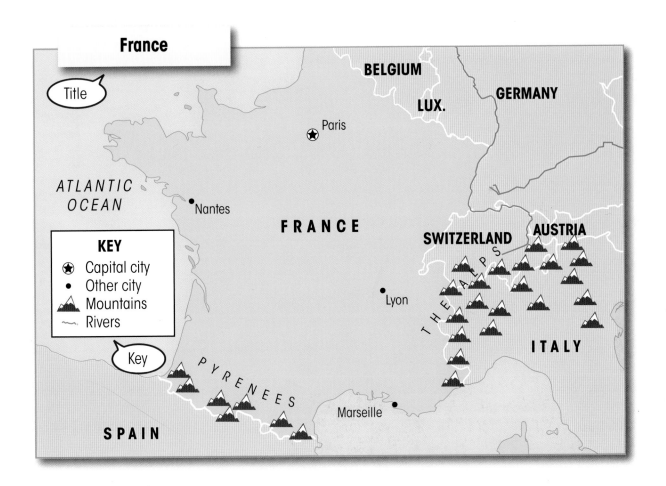

France

Title

BELGIUM

GERMANY

LUX.

Paris

ATLANTIC OCEAN

Nantes

FRANCE

SWITZERLAND AUSTRIA

THE ALPS

KEY
- ⍟ Capital city
- • Other city
- 🏔 Mountains
- ⌇ Rivers

Key

Lyon

ITALY

PYRENEES

Marseille

SPAIN

Using colour

Some maps use colour to show different areas. Countries are often shown with different colours. The map below uses colour to show different buildings.

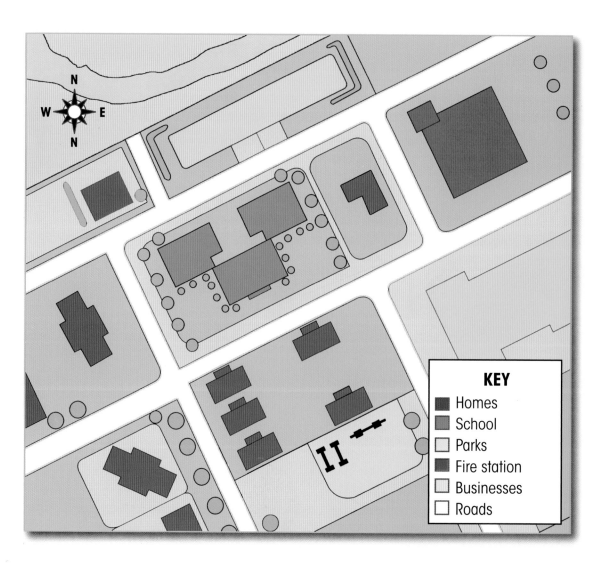

KEY
- Homes
- School
- Parks
- Fire station
- Businesses
- Roads

Scale

Most maps have a **scale**. This feature can be used to measure distance. The scale shows how many kilometres or miles are represented by every centimetre or inch.

You can use the scale to measure distance.

Large and small

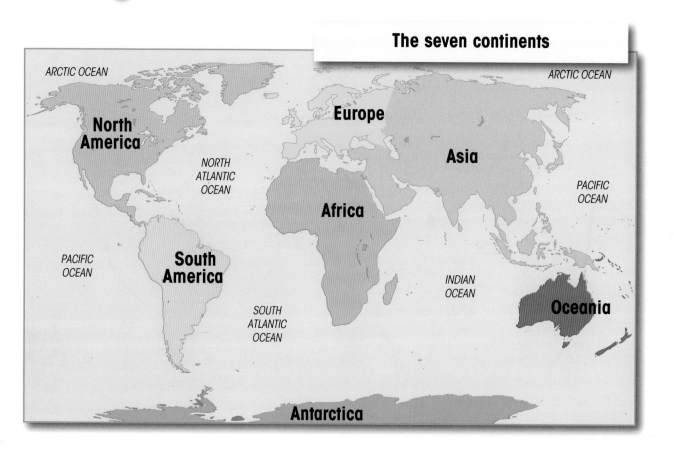

The seven continents

ARCTIC OCEAN

ARCTIC OCEAN

North America

Europe

Asia

NORTH ATLANTIC OCEAN

PACIFIC OCEAN

Africa

PACIFIC OCEAN

South America

INDIAN OCEAN

SOUTH ATLANTIC OCEAN

Oceania

Antarctica

Some maps show a very large area, such as a **continent**. These maps may only show **borders** between countries and large bodies of water.

Some maps show a smaller area, such as a city or town. These maps include many details. They show the location of parks, streets, museums, and hospitals.

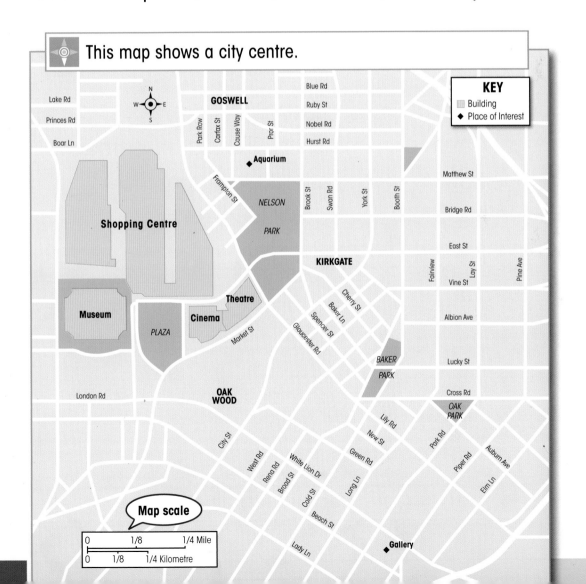

This map shows a city centre.

KEY
☐ Building
◆ Place of Interest

Lines around the world

Some maps have lines on them that divide the world into parts. Two important lines are the **Equator** and the **Prime Meridian**.

The Equator is an imaginary line that runs across the Earth. It is halfway between the North Pole and the South Pole.

The Prime Meridian is an imaginary line that runs from the top to the bottom of the Earth. It goes from the North Pole to the South Pole. Together, these imaginary lines divide the world into four parts.

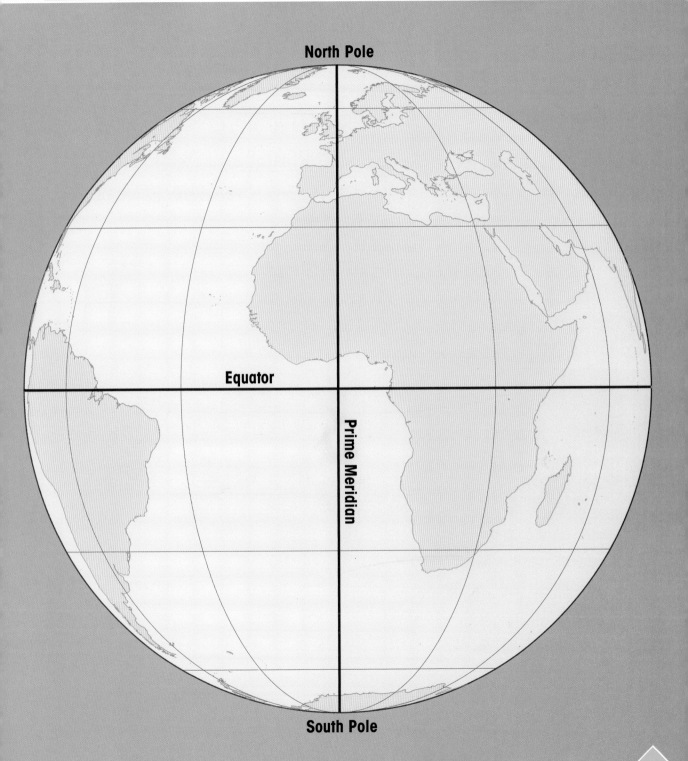

North Pole

Equator

Prime Meridian

South Pole

Map grids

Some maps use a **grid** to help you find the location of a place. A grid has lines that run across the map and up and down the map. All lines are the same distance apart.

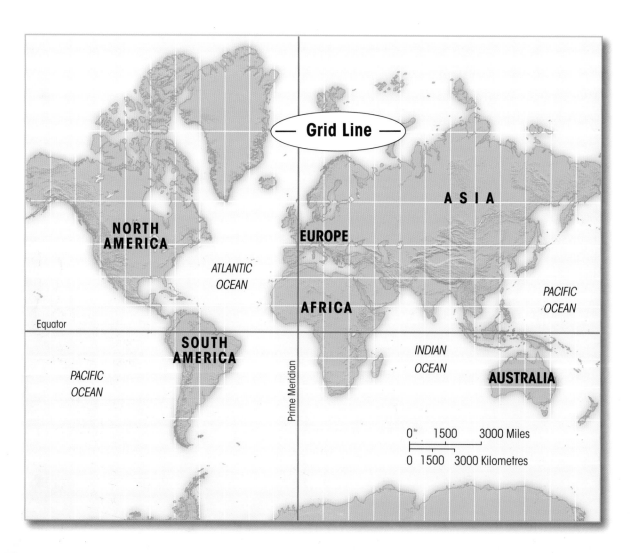

Grid Line

ASIA

NORTH
AMERICA

EUROPE

ATLANTIC
OCEAN

PACIFIC
OCEAN

AFRICA

Equator

SOUTH
AMERICA

INDIAN
OCEAN

AUSTRALIA

PACIFIC
OCEAN

Prime Meridian

0   1500   3000 Miles

0   1500   3000 Kilometres

City maps often have a grid. This type of grid has letters along one side of the map and numbers along the other. The lines from a letter and a number come together to show the exact location of a place.

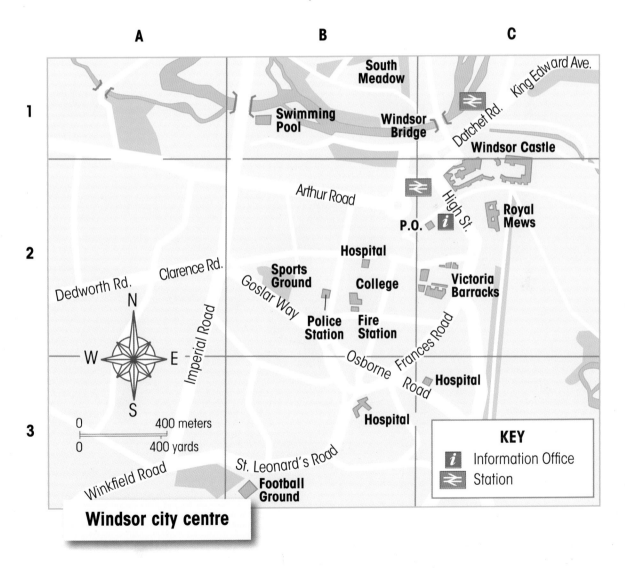

Windsor city centre

Latitude and longitude

A special type of **grid** shows the exact location of places. This grid is called **latitude** and **longitude**.

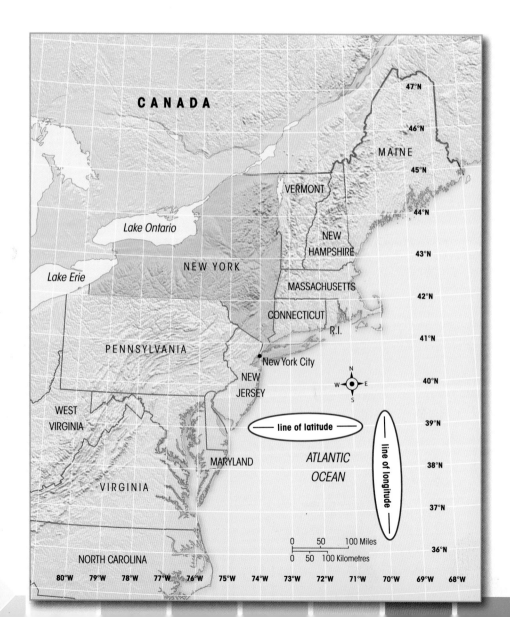

Latitude tells you how far north or south you are from the **Equator**. Latitude lines run across the map. Longitude tells you how far east or west you are from the **Prime Meridian**. Longitude lines run up and down the map.

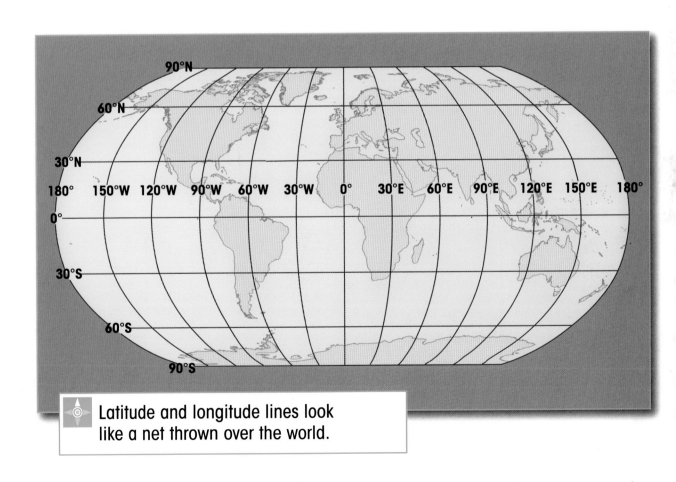

Latitude and longitude lines look like a net thrown over the world.

Making maps

In the past, **cartographers** used special tools to draw maps. Today, they can use computers to help them draw maps. They can also use images from **satellites**. Satellites take pictures of the Earth from space.

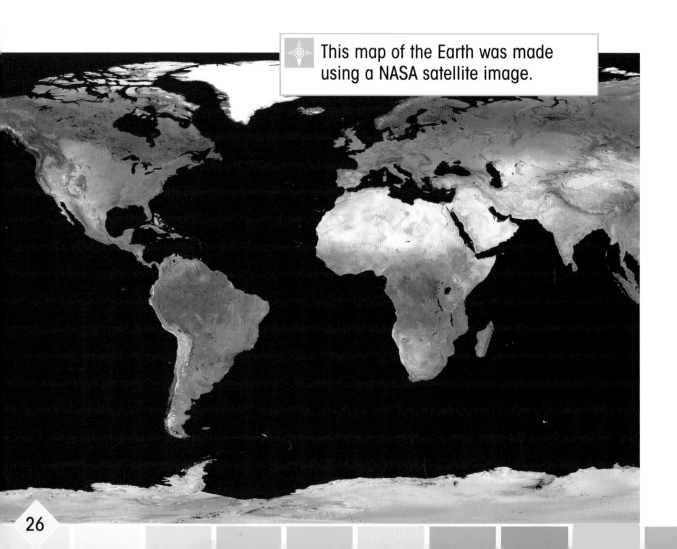

This map of the Earth was made using a NASA satellite image.

Some cars have a GPS that shows driving directions.

Cartographers also use the **Global Positioning System (GPS)**. GPS is a computer network that collects pictures from satellites high above the Earth. GPS can tell people exactly where they are and how to get from one place to another. Mapmakers can also use GPS to draw the exact location of places on a map.

Maps are an important part of our lives. They can show us all kinds of information about the world we live in.

Map activities

Activity 1: Map collection

1. Collect as many different maps as you can. Examples of maps you might be able to collect are bus routes, zoo maps, and city maps.

2. Think about local businesses that may have maps. For example, the bank may have a map that shows where cash machines are located. Your doctor may have a map showing the way to the hospital.

3. Look at the maps and discuss or write down the ways the maps are different and similar. Why do the maps look different?

Activity 2: Create a map

Draw a map of an imaginary place. You may want to create a place of your own, or draw a map about a place in a book that you like. Don't forget to include a title, **key**, **scale**, and **compass rose**.

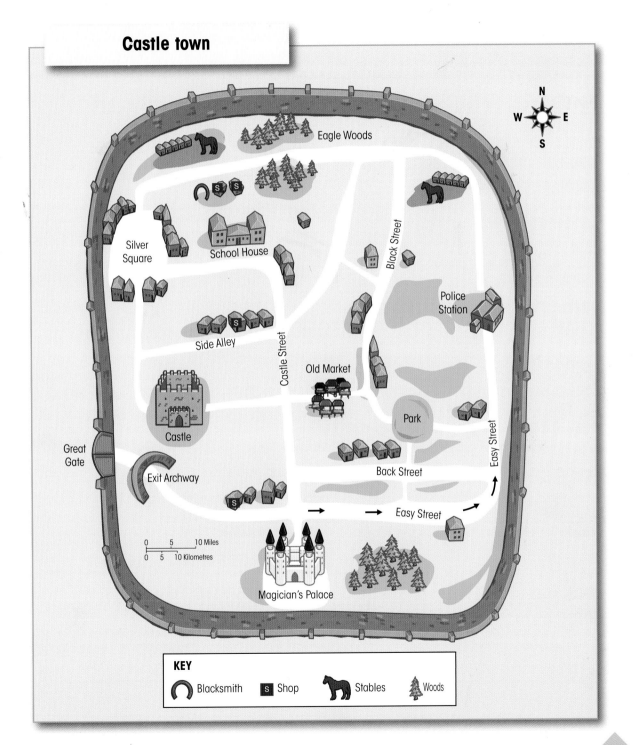

Castle town

Eagle Woods

Silver
Square

School House

Black Street

Police
Station

Side Alley

Castle Street

Old Market

Park

Castle

Easy Street

Great
Gate

Exit Archway

Back Street

Easy Street

0   5   10 Miles

0   5   10 Kilometres

Magician's Palace

KEY

⌒ Blacksmith   Ⓢ Shop   🐎 Stables   🌲 Woods

Glossary

border imaginary line that divides two places

capital city where leaders of a country meet and work

cardinal direction one of the four main directions: north, south, east, or west

cartographer person who makes maps

compass rose symbol on a map that shows direction

continent very large area of land surrounded by water; there are seven continents in the world.

Equator imaginary line that divides the Earth between north and south

grid group of lines that are the same distance apart

Global Positioning System (GPS) group of computers and satellites that work together to show your exact location

key table that shows what the symbols on a map mean

latitude lines on a map that run from east to west

longitude lines on a map that run from north to south

Prime Meridian line that divides the Earth between east and west

satellite object that travels above the Earth and sends information back to the Earth

scale feature on a map that can be used to measure distance

symbol picture that stands for something else

Find out more

Organizations and websites

The websites below may have some advertisements on them. Make sure to ask a trusted adult to look at them with you. You should never give out personal information online, including your name and address, without first talking to a trusted adult.

Google Maps
Visit Google maps (**maps.google.co.uk**) to find directions from your house to places nearby and far away. Try putting in your address and the address of your school. Do the directions given match your route?

National Geographic
National Geographic provides free maps and photos of the Earth, as well as interesting articles about people and animals. Visit **www. nationalgeographic.com**.

Books to read

Heinemann First Atlas, Daniel Block and Marta Segal Block
    (Heinemann Library, 2007)

Inside Access: Maps & Mapping, Jinny Johnson and Lyn Store
    (Kingfisher, 2007)

Maps and Symbols, Susan Lomas (Hodder Wayland, 2004)

Index